COUNTRIES

Australia

Alice Harman

Explore the world with Popcorn - your complete first non-fiction library.

Look out for more titles in the Popcorn range. All books have the same format of simple text and striking images. Text is carefully matched to the pictures to help readers to identify and understand key vocabulary.
www.waylandbooks.co.uk/popcorn

Published in 2013 by Wayland
Copyright © Wayland 2013

Wayland
Hachette Children's Books
338 Euston Road
London NW1 3BH

Wayland Australia
Level 17/207 Kent Street
Sydney NSW 2000

Produced for Wayland by
White-Thomson Publishing Ltd
www.wtpub.co.uk
+44 (0)843 208 7460

Editor: Alice Harman
Designer: Clare Nicholas
Picture researcher: Alice Harman
Series consultant: Kate Ruttle
Design concept: Paul Cherrill

British Library Cataloging in Publication Data
Harman, Alice.
   Australia. -- (Countries)(Popcorn)
   1. Australia--Juvenile literature.
   I. Title II. Series
   919.4-dc23

ISBN: 978 0 7502 7940 6

10 9 8 7 6 5 4 3 2 1

Wayland is a division of Hachette Children's Books,
an Hachette UK company.
www.hachette.co.uk

Printed and bound in China

Picture/Illustration Credits: Alamy: David Hancock 10, Bill Bachman 15, Art Directors & TRIP 17; Peter Bull: 23; Stefan Chabluk: 4; City of Sydney: 20; Corbis: Ludo Kuipers 21; downtoerth hotel: Rose & Alex Morgan 13 inset; Dreamstime: Hlphoto 1/6, Daniel Krzowski 5, OnAir2 10, Peter Wilson 11, Neale Cousland 18, Celso Diniz 22bl, Kaarsten 22br, Maria Feklistova front cover; Shutterstock: EpicStockMedia 2/19, deb22 7, benfischinger 7 inset, Ximagination 8b, Markus Gebauer 8t, deb22 9, Thorsten Rust 12, Martin Horsky 13 b/g, Connie Puntoriero 14t, Neale Cousland 14b, Nejron Photo 16, 2/19, Jeroen Visser 22tr, S.Cooper Digital 22tl; Wikimedia: 22b

 Contents

Where is Australia?

Here is a map of Australia.

Australia is a huge island.

Aboriginal people have been in
Australia for over 40,000 years.

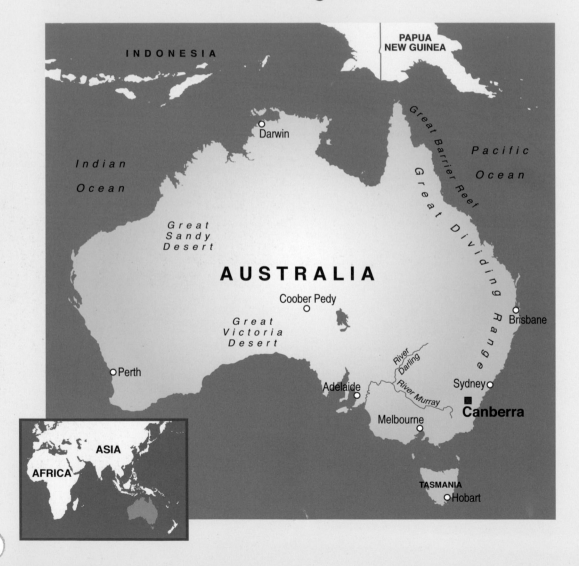

INDONESIA

PAPUA
NEW GUINEA

Darwin

Pacific

Ocean

Indian

Ocean

*Great
Barrier
Reef*

*Great
Sandy
Desert*

Great Dividing Range

AUSTRALIA

Coober Pedy

Brisbane

*Great
Victoria
Desert*

*River
Darling*

Perth

Adelaide

River Murray

Sydney

Canberra

Melbourne

ASIA

AFRICA

TASMANIA

Hobart

Canberra is the capital city,
but Sydney is the biggest and
best-known city in Australia.
Sydney is by the sea.

Bondi Beach is a famous
beach near Sydney.

There are
over 10,000
beaches in
Australia.

Land and sea

The huge area of desert and grassland in central Australia is called the outback. It is very dry and flat, with red earth and enormous rocks.

Eucalyptus trees grow in the outback. Oil from these trees is used in some medicines.

eucalyptus tree

Australia is an island, so there is coast all the way around it. There are coral reefs in the sea along the coast.

The fish that live in these coral reefs are often brightly coloured.

The Great Barrier Reef is the largest coral reef in the world.

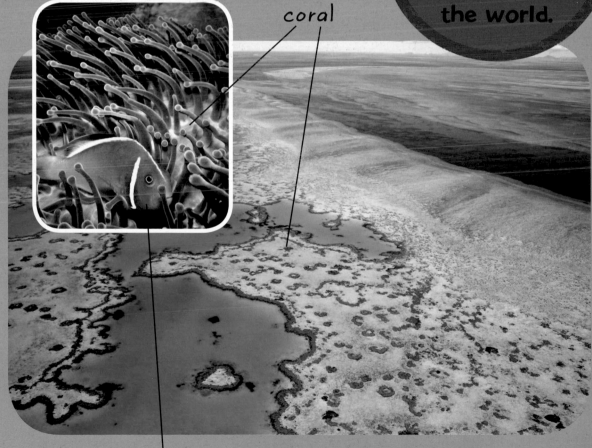

coral

clownfish

The weather

In summer, it is often warm and sunny. But there are sometimes dangerous storms and floods.

▶ A flood in Brisbane, a city in eastern Australia.

▼ A sunny tropical beach near Brisbane.

In the east of Australia, there is a very long mountain range called the Great Dividing Range. Snow falls here in the winter.

People like to go skiing and snowboarding in the mountains.

In Australia, winter is from June to August.

9

Town and country

Most Australians live in cities.
Almost all these cities are
near the coast.

Some children play
and swim in the sea
after school.

The thick forest at the edge of the outback is called the 'bush'. Fires often start in these forests because of the hot, dry weather.

Australia is one of the top five driest countries in the world.

Bush fires can spread for hundreds of miles and burn for weeks.

 # Homes

In cities, many people live in
tall blocks of flats. Hundreds of
people can live in one building.

Flats in Sydney don't often have gardens.
Some flats have balconies instead.

In Coober Pedy, a town in the outback, it gets so hot that some people build homes underground to stay cool.

Underground homes in Australia are called 'dugouts'.

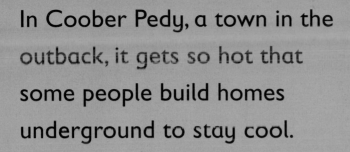

This house is carved into the underground rock.

 Shopping

Big cities in Australia have modern shopping malls. People shop here for clothes, furniture and other goods.

The Queen Victoria shopping centre in Sydney is inside a beautiful old building.

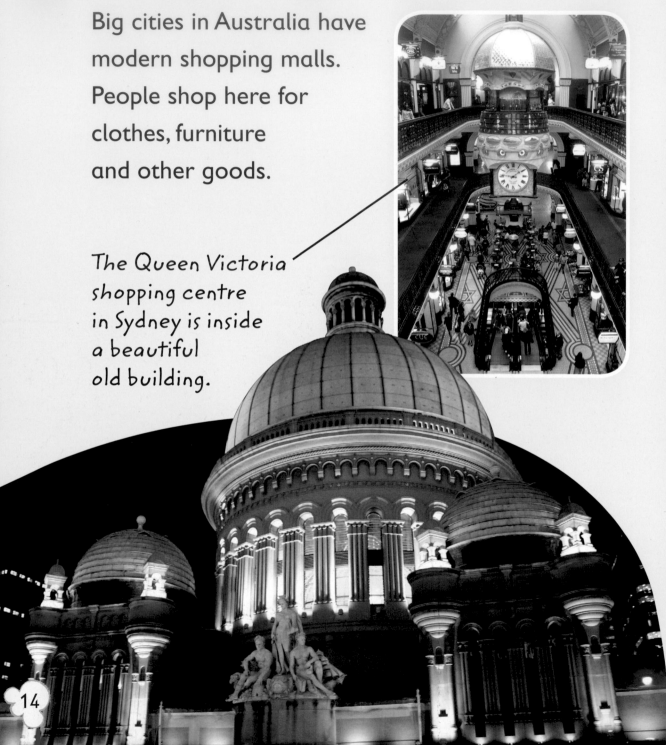

Most towns have a weekly street market where people sell fresh food and hand-made crafts from the local area.

This man is selling traditional Australian didgeridoos and boomerangs.

Food

Australians eat lots of different foods from around the world. Asian and European dishes are popular.

Many Australians eat sushi, a Japanese dish often made with raw fish.

People have barbecues outside, in the garden or on the beach. The most popular foods to cook are meat, fish and prawns.

When eating outside on a sunny day, it is very important to wear suntan lotion.

An Australian burger has beetroot, pineapple and an egg on top!

 # Sport

More than half of Australians play sport at least once a week. The most popular sports to play and watch are Australian football, rugby and cricket.

In Australian football, players can pick up the ball with their hands.

Many Australians love to surf.
Surfers stand on surf boards
to ride large waves into shore.

A surfer needs great balance and strength to stay upright on their board.

Holidays and festivals

The Sydney Harbour firework show on New Year's Eve is one of the biggest in the world.

Some people watch the fireworks from boats out on the water.

Sydney Opera House

The Aboriginal people were the first people to live in Australia. The Barunga Festival in June celebrates their traditional culture.

There are 145 Aboriginal languages in Australia today.

These boys are performing a dance, dressed in traditional clothing.

21

Animals

Australia has many animals that don't live in the wild anywhere else on Earth. Can you name some of them?

koala

sugar glider

emu

kangaroo

echidna

1 = kangaroo
2 = emu
3 = echidna
4 = koala
5 = sugar glider

Make a boomerang

You will need:
- a piece of thick cardboard
- scissors · a black pen
- coloured felt-tip pens

Traditional Australian Aboriginal boomerangs are mostly made out of wood, and often painted with bright colours.

1. Draw this shape on the cardboard and carefully cut it out with scissors.

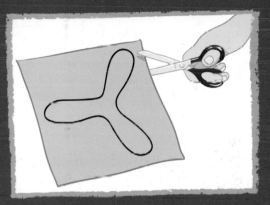

2. Fold the edges as shown in the picture.

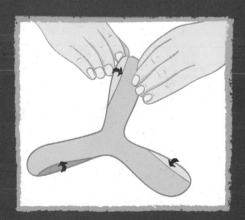

3. Draw colourful patterns on your boomerang with the felt-tip pens.

4. Hold your boomerang flat between your fingers and thumb, and throw it away from you. Then watch it come back!

Glossary

Aboriginal Aboriginal people were the first people to live in Australia

balcony an outdoor area on the side of a building, with a wall around it

barbecue a grill for cooking food, usually used outside

boomerang a curved flat piece of wood that comes back to you when you throw it

capital the city where the government of the country meets

coral reef an underwater shelf made of corals, sea animals with hard outsides

didgeridoo a long wooden musical instrument, which people play by blowing into it

flood when lots of rain makes water rise and cover land that is usually dry

goods things that people can buy

outback the huge area of desert and grassland in central Australia

snowboarding a sport in which people stand on a board and slide down a snowy hill

Index